These Are My Senses

What Can I Feel?

Joanna Issa

Raintree is an imprint of Capstone Global Library Limited, a company incorporated in England and Wales having its registered office at 7 Pilgrim Street, London, EC4V 6LB – Registered company number: 6695582

www.raintreepublishers.co.uk
myorders@raintreepublishers.co.uk

Text © Capstone Global Library Limited 2015
First published in hardback in 2014
Published in paperback 2015
The moral rights of the proprietor have been asserted.

Edited by Siân Smith
Designed by Richard Parker and Peggie Carley
Picture research by Tracy Cummins
Production by Victoria Fitzgerald
Originated by Capstone Global Library Ltd
Printed and bound in China

ISBN 978 1 406 28369 3 (hardback)
18 17 16 15 14
10 9 8 7 6 5 4 3 2 1

ISBN 978 1 406 28375 4 (paperback)
19 18 17 16 15
10 9 8 7 6 5 4 3 2 1

British Library Cataloguing in Publication Data
A full catalogue record for this book is available from the British Library.

Acknowledgements
We would like to thank the following for permission to reproduce photographs: Getty Images: Photodisc/© JuanSilva 2010, 17; iStock: © JCREATION, 8, © moxiegirl12, 11, back cover, © Salima Senyavskaya, 14, © will_snyder, 7; Shutterstock: © auremar, 19, © Dhoxax, 12, © Diana Taliun, 16, 20 left, © George Lamson, 4, © Igor Kovalchuk, 15, 21 left, © ipag, 6, © Monika Gniot, 13, © oksix, 18, 21 right, © Sunny Forest, 10, © vidguten, 5, 22 left, © Whitear, 9, 20 right, 22 right.

Cover photograph reproduced with permission of Getty Images, LWA/Dann Tardif.

Every effort has been made to contact copyright holders of material reproduced in this book. Any omissions will be rectified in subsequent printings if notice is given to the publisher.

Contents

What can I feel? 4

Quiz: Opposite pairs 20

Picture glossary 22

Index 22

Notes for teachers
and parents. 23

In this book 24

What can I feel?

Here is a puppy.

It feels **soft**.

Here is some bubble gum.

It feels sticky.

Here is a cactus.

It feels **spiky**.

Here is a tree.

It feels rough.

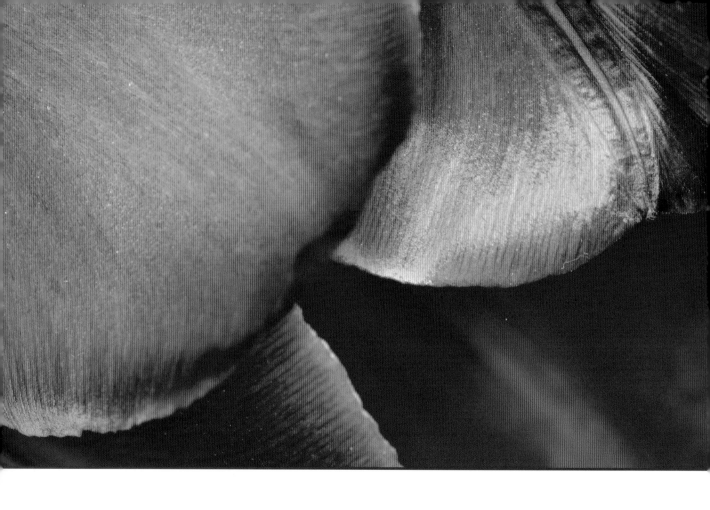

Here is a flower.

It feels smooth.

Here is a leaf.

It feels rough.

Here is play dough.

It feels soft.

Here is honey.

It feels sticky.

Quiz: Opposite pairs

Which of these objects
feels spiky?

Which of these objects feels sticky?

The cactus feels spiky.
The honey feels sticky.

21

Picture glossary

 soft

 spiky

Index

bubble gum 6

cactus 8

flower 12

honey 18

leaf 14

play dough 16

puppy 4

tree 10

Notes for teachers and parents

BEFORE READING

Building background:

Ask children to think of things that are soft to touch and things that are rough.
Which do they like to feel best?

AFTER READING

Recall and reflection:

What things are soft to touch (puppy, play dough)? What things are sticky (honey, bubble gum)? Would children like to touch something sticky? Why or why not?

Sentence knowledge:

Ask children to look at page 12. How many sentences are on this page?
How can they tell?

Word knowledge (phonics):

Encourage children to point at the word *feels* on page 13. Sound out the four phonemes in the word *f/ee/l/s.* Ask children to sound out each phoneme as they point at the letters and then blend the sounds together to make the word *feels.* Challenge them to say some words that rhyme with *feels* (heels, meals, peels, wheels).

Word recognition:

Ask children to point to the word *rough* on page 11. Can they also find it on page 15?

EXTENDING IDEAS

Put a number of small objects in a bag (toy car, wooden brick, soft toy, pencil, rubber, sock). Ask children to put their hands inside the bag and feel for an object. Can they describe how it feels to the other children? Can the other children guess what the object is? Let children pull the object out of the bag to show the class if they were right or wrong.

In this book

Topic

touch and senses

High-frequency words

a

here

is

it

Sentence stems

1. It feels _____.
2. Here is a _____.